Real Estate: Blueprint to Success

Flipping Houses, Home Buying, and Rental Properties

By

ALAN ANDERSON

Alan Anderson

© Copyright 2018 – All rights reserved.

Real Estate

In no way is it legal to reproduce, duplicate, or transmit any part of this document in either electronic means or in printed format. Recording of this publication is strictly prohibited, and any storage of this document is not allowed unless with written permission from the publisher. All rights reserved.

The information provided herein is stated to be truthful and consistent in that any liability, in terms of inattention or otherwise, by any usage or abuse of any policies, processes, or directions contained within, is the solitary and utter responsibility of the recipient reader. Under no circumstances will any legal responsibility or blame be held against the publisher for any reparation, damage, or monetary loss due to the information herein, either directly or indirectly.

Respective authors own all copyrights not held by the publisher.

Legal Notice:

This book is copyright protected. This is only for personal use. You cannot amend, distribute, sell, use, quote, or paraphrase any part or the content within this book without the consent of the author or copyright owner. Legal action will be pursued if this is breached.

Disclaimer Notice:

Please note the information contained within this document is for educational and entertainment purposes only. Every attempt has been made to provide accurate, up-to-date, reliable, and complete information. No warranties of any kind are expressed or implied. Readers acknowledge that the author is not engaging in the rendering of legal, financial, medical, or professional advice.

Alan Anderson

Table of Contents

Introduction 7

Chapter 1 – Looking for Property 9

Chapter 2 – What to Look for in a Home 15

Chapter 3 – Finance and Offers 19

    Cash Buying 20

    Making Offers 20

Chapter 4 – Rental or Sale? 23

Chapter 5 – Repairing and Flipping a Home 27

    Ripping out Tiling, Bathrooms, and Kitchens 27

    Flooring 27

    First Fix, Second Fix, and Finishing 28

    Selling or Renting the Property 28

Conclusion 31

Alan Anderson

Introduction

Many people do not realize the amount of money that can be made from real estate. They see it on TV in such shows as Property Brothers, where homes are bought at low prices and then renovated to make them much more valuable and serve as dream homes for others, but they don't see that there are savvy investors who are actually managing to make a living from this – and a very good one at that. This book gives you the lowdown on making money from flipping houses.

It also gives you a lot more than that and acts as a blueprint for your home buying and selling business, aside from showing you how to make a killing on rental property. There is a fortune waiting for those who do this correctly, while those who dabble in flipping homes may fall by the wayside. The trick is to know when to buy, what to buy, and how to go about renovating and using the property in the best way possible.

This book gives you all of the information you need to know so that you don't make mistakes, and if you have been thinking about flipping homes as a means to earn your living, it's time to read the blueprint, to see your dream in black and white, and to adhere to it. That's when it's possible to make real money.

Just having sufficient money to buy one fixer upper can put you on the trail to success or failure, depending upon your ability to follow the blueprint to the letter. See the warning signs. See the points that make a home a strong investment. Step in at the right time with all the right information, and you, too, can join the successful businessmen who actually do make a lot of money building people's dream homes.

Alan Anderson

Whether you opt for rental properties or for properties that are sold outright depends on several factors, as you will see during the course of reading this blueprint to success. You can make property the best investment that you ever made. There are stumbling blocks. There are disadvantages, but if you already know what these are, you can be miles ahead of the competition and still make a killing. This book is based on extensive experience in flipping houses and cashing in on the rental market. Success for life is something everyone seeks, and the investment you make now could be just what you are looking for to secure your future.

Real Estate

Attention Real Estate Investors, Wholesalers, & Agents!

"Customize A Deal-Finding System That Creates A Virtually ENDLESS Supply Of Below Market-Value Real Estate Investing Opportunities"

And Discover How You Can Automate The Entire Process!

If you've wasted hours online looking for great deals on investment properties...
and wished there was a better and faster way to do it...
Then your prayers have just been answered!

www.northstarreaders.com/real-estate-deals

Alan Anderson

Chapter 1 – Looking for Property

If you decide that you would like to join the many that are already flipping houses, you need to study your market. Buying a house and doing it up without knowing what the market is doing in a particular area is foolhardy and risky. There are cheap properties out there, but before you can really tell if something is cheap, you have to know current market values in the geographical area where you are looking. Don't make the mistake of taking asking prices in the local newspapers as being the correct price. These are asking prices. They are not the prices that are being realized. Visit real estate agents to find out what is actually selling and for what price so that you have a guide, but go further than that.

Look for Short Sales

These are houses that are sold quickly because the lender wants his money back when a homeowner hasn't paid the mortgage on time and the house is repossessed. The lender doesn't care about the value of the home. What they care about is getting their money back, and sometimes, these homes are the best bargain you can possibly wish to get. Look out for property auctions as well as often, these are places where bargains can be had. Before you invest a buck, observe. You need to see what kinds of houses are on the market, but you also need to know what kind of market that house is in.

Alan Anderson

Rental Investment or Flipping Investment?

In an area where rental property is in short supply, you can make a killing on rentals, but you will need to know in advance what kind of property is needed within the area in which you intend to buy. For example, is the local university looking for rental property because of shortage of accommodation? Are there businesses that seek short-term rentals on a regular basis for visiting executives? The only way you are going to know about this is to get out there and knock on doors. Knowing your market helps you to establish whether the area is popular with renters or is more likely to be snapped up by owners.

Owning a property isn't just a case of seeing a home and buying it. You have to offer what the market needs. For example, families will buy homes in rural areas if there is sufficient access to good services, such as schools, shops, and transport to get to work. However, uptown property is a highly sought after commodity if you choose an area where homes are in short supply. So what's the problem? You have to compete with other properties, so know what you are competing against before you start to get out there and spend money. Know who is likely to buy the home, because tailoring your home to a specific market is a very wise way to go. Students from the local university will have different needs from visiting executives. First-time buyers may be looking for homes they can expand their lives into, while families with children will be looking for accommodation that is flexible enough to fit their needs.

The equation is fairly simple. You need to know who wants what in which particular area and then balance that against what is available and how that can be brought up to date and sold when placed on the market against competition. If you get

Real Estate

this part of the equation right, there's a whole load of money to be made. If you get it wrong, you may find you'll be lucky to break even.

When you look for property, compare prices with other properties in the area. Look for homes that seem cheaper than normal, but don't let the search stop there. Another great indication that the seller will come down in price is if the house has been on the market for a while. You also need to look into the aspects that are shown in the next chapter, but for now, shortlist homes that are of interest so that you have something to go by.

Make sure that you have the money ready for a purchase, whether that means finance or ash. Those who have financing ready can use that as bait when making offers because ready money talks louder than promises. The style of home should be within your level of expertise. If it is too large a task, don't touch it. Shortlisting those homes that may be of interest is always a good idea. At the same time, keep an eye on properties that are new to the market and auctions as and when they come up. You need to keep your eye on this ever-changing market if you want to make an impact at exactly the right moment.

Be sure to have your list ready for viewing so that you can get a feel for the market in your particular area. Your shortlist of houses needs time for inspection and examination to see if they are viable for either rental or sales at a profit. Find out the kind of rents that are achieved in your area because this makes a huge difference in whether you decide to sell or to invest long term in property ownership. If you do decide to go toward renting property, know what you are likely to get for each unit rented. Being informed keeps you ahead of the game and helps you to make the right investments. Some rentals will actually help you to finance other projects, while some will merely be monthly income to pay mortgages. You need to decide at this point which way you think you would like to go.

Chapter 2 – What to Look for in a Home

There is a difference between a home that has been empty for a while and a home that has been neglected. Learn the difference. The telltale signs are there. An empty property may feel cold and a little unkempt, but a neglected property will have all kinds of jobs left undone. The problem with buying neglected property is that you never know what you are going to uncover when you start to strip the place back. An empty property that looks like it was cared for is a far better bet.

When looking at properties, you need to assess the following:

- Are you going to knock walls down?
- Does the property need to be reconfigured?
- Will you have to update the electrical system?
- What's the heating system like, and is it working?
- Do the kitchen and bathrooms need to be updated?
- Will plumbing work need to be done?

These are immediate concerns that cost money, and you need to know that you have the trades available to do your work in a timely fashion. Remember that each day of ownership is a day longer that you have your money tied up and that you have to meet household bills. This can eat into your profits, so you need tradesmen you can trust.

If you have doubts about things being up to code, it may be worthwhile making an offer subject to satisfactory inspections for the following:

- Electrical installation
- Heating
- Termites
- Wood rot
- Rising Damp

Some of the problems that you find in properties only become apparent once you have stripped back the façade, and that's when money gets eaten up very quickly. Thus, you need as much information as you can get about the place. Sometimes, it pays to buy a home that has been gutted, because at least you know upon what foundation you are building. Look also for problems with footings or slipped walls because these can be very costly to put right. The roof is important as well. I tend to look for houses with solid foundations, good walls, and a good roof and then work from there. Sometimes, old flooring is hidden beneath carpet. Try to lift an area in a corner to see what's underneath because you really can do a house up using the old floors if they have always been covered with carpets.

Look for the outside appeal of the property because this is what sells a home. If you can't do anything about it because of neighboring properties, chances are you won't find the same kind of price found in a neighborhood where owners take pride in their homes. Make yourself a checklist, and be sure to look at everything. It's easy to get emotional about a property, but if you are going into business, you have to forget about your own personal preferences, as these may not be relevant in the market. Think of the home as a potential home for the right kind of people that you are targeting.

The blueprint for flipping homes depends upon being observant, being aware of what it will cost you to remedy problems, and having a great team of workers who can help you to get that house up to scratch. Are ceilings flat? If they are not, perhaps they need structural support, and that's costly. If you intend to make a home into apartments, for example, is there access for each independent unit, or will this mean structural work?

When you are looking at homes, be sure to take masses of photographs. Then, if you can't get the tradesmen to the property, you can take your pictures to them to get an idea of costs before you actually part with your money. That's a very useful tool. I remember one house where the electrical installation was not that clever, and I photographed everything because my electrician wasn't available on the day, and I saved myself a lot of expense by doing so.

The house that is on the market may not be someone's dream home now, but could you make it into that dream home? Do you have sufficient expertise at your fingertips to have a fairly quick turnover? You also need to check at this time what the rules are on flipping houses within your area and whether there is any capital gains tax on your profits. In some regions, it's better to invest in one huge project than to take on many smaller ones because of this aspect. Find out from your local accountant, because this is vital to know before making an offer. Usually, this applies after you have bought a set number of homes that are not going to be used as your principal residence, but it may not apply where you live. However, you do need to know, as it will affect your profits.

Alan Anderson

Chapter 3 – Finance and Offers

If you borrow money to flip houses, you cause yourself a problem in one way. Every day that the money is not repaid, you have to pay interest. You may buy a house at $100,000, but you also need to work out what it actually costs you given the time that the property is stagnant during repairs. It isn't going to give you income at this time, and it is still going to cost you money. Find out about loans that have no penalty if you pay back early because they may be much more viable. By talking to your bank in advance, you can come up with a figure that they are prepared to advance and that gives you your purchase price.

The money that you have also has to pay for all of the repairs to the home to make it a viable proposition to a prospective purchaser. Thus, if you buy a home under list price at $99,000, and there are repairs that are estimated at £100,000, you need to be sure that a house that is in perfect order will fetch a price of more than $199,000 because if it won't, you need to walk away. You will have broken even, but that's not what flipping houses is all about. You need a profit margin. Thus, when calculating the price you can afford, add up the following:

- Price of house
- Price of potential repairs and refurbishment
- Contingency (for hidden costs)

I usually add a contingency of 35 percent because that's a pretty safe figure if you have looked into all of the potential for the home and are just worried about things you may find when you start to strip the home.

Cash Buying

Cash buying means that you have the money ready, even if this is borrowed. A cash buyer is someone who can produce cash on the day of purchase and will always be preferred over a purchaser who has not yet arranged finance. Put yourself into that bracket by having assurance from the bank in writing that you are good for the amount of money you need.

Making Offers

When you are making offers for a home, you need to bear in mind what it will cost you to put the home back to a good selling proposition. Thus, if the home is up for sale at $150,000, and you need £50,000 for repairs, you need to try and knock the price down to take account of the current market value of houses in that area, less the repairs and less your contingency. Go in on the low side without insulting the vendor. In this case, I would approach the vendor to discuss the offer rather than go through an agent. If the agent wants to be present, that's okay, but you need to get your point over, and when a vendor meets you and sees that you are sincere, all kinds of good things can happen.

Explain that you have estimates on repairs and that you are offering the low price to take account of this. Explain also that you're not made of money and that you don't want to spend so

Real Estate

much on repairs to bring the house up to spec if that cost goes beyond what the current market value is. The seller will see that what you say makes sense but may still counter your initial offer. However, having rapport with a seller puts you at a decided advantage.

You can learn the reasons for selling, and that helps you to know how desperate the seller is to sell the house:

- Has it been on the market for a while?
- Is the property for sale because a relationship has ended?
- Has someone died?

Often, if you know why the house is for sale, this also gives you an indication as to how quickly the seller wants that house to go. Holding on to a home after a death or a divorce can be painful for people, and they are often willing to let the home go for less than it's worth just to get rid of the emotional attachment. If the house has been on the market for a while, the people who do not live there anymore will want to get rid of their monthly outgoings on the house because all the time it's theirs, they are paying. Newly listed properties, on the other hand, are unlikely to go much below list price because the sellers are ever hopeful of maximizing the amount that they can get and haven't yet tested the market.

If you make a bid at an auction, be sure that you don't get carried away. It's very easy to pay over the odds for a home when you get into a bidding race. Remember what your top price is, and stick to it. There will always be other houses, and it's better to walk away with your finances intact than to buy expensively and then try to refurbish the home on an already stretched budget.

Alan Anderson

Chapter 4 – Rental or Sale?

There are several criteria for deciding whether you want to buy homes to sell or to rent. In the early days of flipping houses, you will need cash from one project to finance the next; thus, buying houses that will be done up and then selling it to pay for the next project is the most sensible way forward. However, you may be presented with an opportunity that is too good to miss in the rental area. For example, if you were to see a home for sale that lends itself to being split into separate units for rental, can you afford to wait for your capital investment to be paid back? One way that people do this is to work out the monthly price of the mortgage and then to work out what the likely rental will be on each of the units. It's important to know that there is demand for rental property in the area where the house is located.

If you borrow money to buy the home, then the rental that you get may actually pay off the mortgage, so your investment is long term, and your tenants pay your debt to the bank. If the property price is too excessive, then the rental may not cover what you borrowed, so you need to toss up, based on the figures, which kind of investment gives you the better return.

House Costs

| Rental House | $100,000 @ 5 percent over 30 years | Monthly payment = $536

Rental for the property comes in at $800 a month = profit |
|---|---|---|
| Selling home | $100,000 @ 5 percent over 10 year period | Monthly payment: $1060 until the date of sale – thus, add this to sale price to make profit and pay your mortgage costs. Also add setting up charge. |

There are two ways to look at it. If you buy for rental, your tenant pays your mortgage, but your capital is tied up longer. Is the bank prepared to finance your next project while this project is still unpaid for? When buying a home to refurbish and sell, you can actually add your mortgage costs to the sale to ensure that you get your money plus profits. The rental way is good if you have ready cash because it's a way of making money long term and not having to have monthly costs. Instead, you have rental coming in, which can finance a mortgage on a second project.

I was always told not to start a business like this — with debt — and that was sound advice. If you can start with sufficient capital to finance your first project, this first project can actually finance your future projects, and you keep the ball rolling so that, at any given time, you have a project on the go, and its finance comes from the last job that you did.

Rentals can work out to be very beneficial, especially in an area where there is a need for rental property, and you have the money to put into providing tenants with reasonable accommodation. However, if the house is too dilapidated and will cost you more than you have, the rental will only begin to give you money once it has paid for the work that you have already done.

Only you can make your mind up on which way to go, but a clear blueprint is given when you adhere to investment of cash in rental property and then using the money gained from tenants to finance future projects. Yes, there is also money to be had from buying a house cheaply on a loan, but it will be harder to make a profit, bearing in mind that loans cost money. You need to be certain that when the house is done up, it will fetch a good price that will pay back those costs.

The figures above are based on certain percentages, but of course, these differ from time to time, and you need to check them with the bank at the time you are considering buying a home. Knowing what finance is available to you at what cost is essential. You may even find that the bank is prepared to advance your money in stages as and when the equity in the property improves because of the work that has been done. This helps you to keep on track and to keep your budget intact.

Investigating both ways is vital to your success, as one way may be ideal for your start up and give you the experience you need to set up your next investment. However, this depends on your expertise, the reliability of your workforce, and the prices at which you can buy your supplies. Talk to local outlets to find out what discounts are available on important and costly items, such as drywall, plumbing, kitchen units, bathtubs, and furniture. The more you can save, the more you can make in profit.

Chapter 5 – Repairing and Flipping a Home

Whether you flip the home into the rental market or the sale market, as soon as you have the keys, you need to arrange for the work to start without any delay at all. Ripping out all parts of the old home that needs to be replaced will be the first task. Labor isn't that expensive for tasks that don't require specialization, but if you use laborers, be sure that you are there to supervise the work being done, and be very specific about what that work is.

Ripping out Tiling, Bathrooms, and Kitchens

When you do this for either a rental or a sale, remember to salvage whatever you can. For example, kitchen units may be salvageable by replacing doors. However, do bear in mind that purchasers or even renters will expect to see a clean and up-to-date kitchen and bathroom, so these areas need to look clean and tidy.

Flooring

When stripping back carpet to reveal great original flooring, do look to see whether taking down walls will affect the flow of the flooring because, sometimes, this can involve a lot more cost than you anticipated if there are gaps where the walls were built before the floors were laid. Often, you are lucky and find that the walls were added later. If you are going to be in the renovation business, use this as a carrot when buying flooring because this is a commodity that you will need in all of your houses, and if you can strike a deal with a local supplier, this may bring the cost down.

First Fix, Second Fix, and Finishing

This is a hard job for people new to flipping houses. You need to program your workforce so that different trades are not getting in each other's way and so that everything is done in order without electricians and plumbers having to charge waiting time. All of your electrical fittings and plumbing items, such as bath, shower, etc., should be ready for the tradesmen to do their work. When the final finishing is being done, the last thing you need is for a tradesman to want to punch holes in a wall. Work your schedule in a logical fashion.

Selling or Renting the Property

You will need to have the house ready for viewers, regardless of whether you are renting or selling. That means presenting it in the best way possible. If that means hiring a few props, such as furniture items, then it's worth it because people cannot imagine their lives within an empty space. Choose small double beds for small bedrooms. You really can make the space look bigger by the choices that you make. On the day of viewing, have the home ready in neutral shades so that buyers or renters can actually imagine their lives in the house or apartment. It's vital that you work to a good standard because otherwise, you may compromise your reputation for future projects.

All of the effort put in is worth it if you follow the blueprint laid out in this book. You will have become familiar with the market and will have bought a house at a good price that reflects its current condition. The turnover period has to be very quick to save costs, not in terms of the quality of work but in the loans used to secure the property. Thus, always use good quality products, and hire good tradesmen who you know to be reliable.

Alan Anderson

Conclusion

Flipping houses is a great way to invest your money if you have the "savoir faire" and are able to keep an eye on your renovation budget. Often, persons get carried away with the renovations and overspend, but this all eats into profits. If you really want to provide quality accommodation for people, you need to know the kind of people you are marketing to, and your property should meet their requirements.

It's a great life, and it's a very independent way to go. Having flipped more than a dozen houses, I can say that when you achieve the sale at the price that you want, you do feel a certain sense of satisfaction. You also get the same buzz when your first rental money arrives, but do remember that there will be taxes to pay on the profits and that what you actually get in your hands at the end of the day should still be enough to carry on with the next project. Hiring a good accountant will certainly prove beneficial because he or she will know all the financial rules that apply to flipping houses.

Finally, I'd like to ask you a favor if I may. If you enjoyed this book, then I'd really appreciate you leaving a review and your feedback on Amazon. You can do that by writing in your Amazon account under Your Orders.

All the best!

Alan Anderson

Real Estate

Attention Real Estate Investors, Wholesalers, & Agents!

"Customize A Deal-Finding System That Creates A Virtually ENDLESS Supply Of Below Market-Value Real Estate Investing Opportunities"

And Discover How You Can Automate The Entire Process!

If you've wasted hours online looking for great deals on investment properties...
and wished there was a better and faster way to do it...
Then your prayers have just been answered!

www.northstarreaders.com/real-estate-deals

WOULDN'T IT BE GREAT IF YOU COULD WATCH YOUR OWN MONEY GROW ITSELF TO EXPONENTIAL PROPORTIONS?

Investing is your friend. While the prospect of dabbling into investments may seem difficult for beginners or even those who have some knowledge, the rewards can be amazing. This book will teach you how to begin investing like a pro through detailed strategies and techniques.

Here's what's in store for you:

- Investing basics for those just starting to get their feet wet
- Investing in stocks and options
- Investing in bonds and mutual funds
- Investing in ETFs and precious metals
- Investing in dividend stocks
- Compare different stock markets
- Find a strategy that's right for you
- Maximize your income potential
- And much more!

Visit to Order Your Copy Today!
https://www.amazon.com/dp/1517050863

TODAY IS THE DAY, TAKE CHARGE OF YOUR TEAM!

The idea behind writing this book was to use my experience to help those starting out and to be able to give useful and sound advice. There are many corporate style books on leadership. What makes mine different is that it's written by someone who has been where you are currently standing, and who understands your difficulty with being faced with the job of team leader for the first time. Walk through the pages and learn how it's done. It's actually easier than you may imagine, once you know what it is that you need to be doing.

In this book you will learn how to:

- Effectively communicate with your team
- Allocate and delegate
- Identify your teams strengths and weaknesses
- Develop your coaching skills
- Manage conflict resolution
- Improve your coaching skills
- Become a great leader
- And much, much more

Visit to Order Your Copy Today!

https://www.amazon.com/dp/1518821782

www.ingramcontent.com/pod-product-compliance
Lightning Source LLC
Chambersburg PA
CBHW07084522O526
45466CB00002B/892